THE SEA

First published 2022 by order of the Tate Trustees by Tate Publishing,
a division of Tate Enterprises Ltd, Millbank, London SW1P 4RG
www.tate.org.uk/publishing

A catalogue record for this book is available from the British Library
ISBN 978 1 84976 827 6

Distributed in the United States and Canada by ABRAMS, New York

Library of Congress Control Number applied for

Senior Editor: Alice Chasey
Series Editor: James Finch
Production: Juliette Dupire
Picture Researcher: Roz Hill
Designed by Narrate + Kelly Barrow
Colour reproduction by DL Imaging, London
Printed in Wales by Cambrian Printers

Front cover: Colin Self, *Power and Beauty No. 2* 1968 (detail, see p.38)
Measurements of artworks are given in centimetres, height before width, before depth.

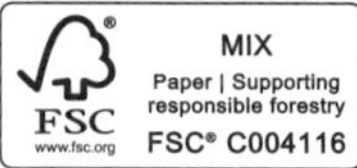

THE SEA

PHILIP HOARE

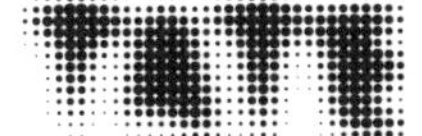

Director's Statement

'Look Again' is a bold new publishing programme from Tate Publishing and Tate Britain. In these books, we are providing a platform for some of the most exciting contemporary voices writing today to explore the national collection of British art in their own way, and reconnect art to our lives today. The books have been developed ahead of the rehang of Tate Britain's collection, which will be launched in 2023 and will foreground many of the artworks discussed here. In this second set of texts – *The Sea* by Philip Hoare, *Complicity* by Jay Bernard, *Fashion* by Shahidha Bari and *Visibility* by Johny Pitts – we are offered unique perspectives on a wide range of artworks across British history, and encouraged to look closely, and to look again.

Alex Farquharson, Director, Tate Britain

Where did the sea begin? In the past, or in our heads? How can we talk about something that has no colour, form or shape of its own, only an echo of the clouds or the sky? The sea defines our weather, supplies our food and every other breath we take. It's the greatest living space on our planet, yet we turn our backs on it every day. 'The sea, everywhere the sea, and no one looking at it', as the Haitian-Canadian writer Dany Laferrière said.

We ignore the sea at the peril of our souls, William Blake intimates, quite ferociously, in his unforgettable image of Isaac Newton perched on the sea bed. The seventeenth-century scientist, whom Blake distrusted, is clearly more concerned with measuring his theories than witnessing the wonders of the deep. He is unaware that an uncanny light has fallen on him; that the vast waters are swirling about over his head; he is even ignorant of the glowing, jewel-like organisms that stud his rocky seat. He's a prisoner of the Enlightenment, 'mad with unbelief', as Peter Ackroyd wrote in his biography of Blake. In his attempt to assess the physical world, Newton has forsaken greater, metaphysical truths.

Blake's contemporaries, Romantic poets such as Byron, Shelley and Keats, knew that without the profundity of the sea, their art would not exist.

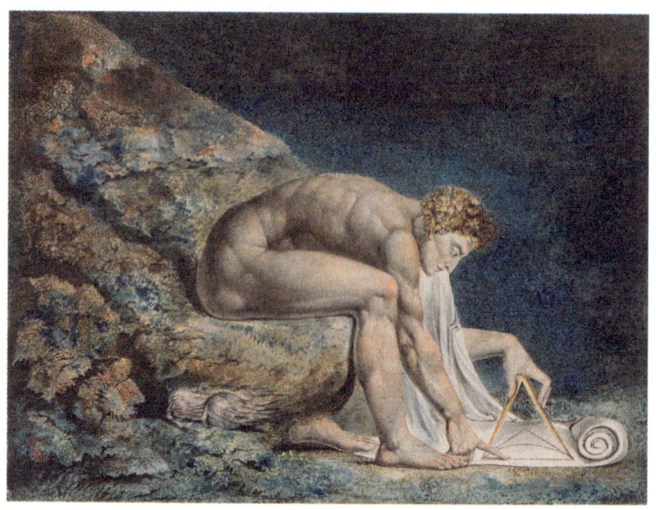

William Blake, *Newton* 1795–c.1805, ink and watercolour on paper, 46 x 60, Tate

'Roll on, thou deep and dark blue ocean – roll!' Byron exhorted; Keats asked for his epitaph to read 'Here lies one whose name was writ in water'; and Shelley, who could not swim, nevertheless liked to try and sink to the bottom, telling his rescuers; 'in another minute I might have been in another planet'.

Much as the poets tried, you can't put your arms around the sea. Yet we call it a body of water, and it is tugged away from us twice daily, tidally, by a foreign body, the moon, which Shakespeare called a watery star. The sea marks our place in time and space. It's where we came from and we're drawn to it, as if to our own natural history. After all, we all came to consciousness in the salty amniotic sea of our mother's womb.

I was born and brought up by the sea, but was so scared of it that I never learned to swim till I was thirty years old. It was the best lesson I ever received, and it took place in Haggerston Baths in the landlocked East End of London.

It wasn't a good start: the turquoise tiles of the municipal pool put me off with their sickly imitation of the sea, as did the sticking plasters and clumps of hair bobbing on its floor. But as I floundered about in the shallow end, an elderly lady in a rubber hat and a trim one-piece swimsuit paused in her stately progress to take pity on me. She taught me to put my face in the water. It was a transformative moment; I bless that aquatic goddess every day. Now, living on the south coast of England, I swim in the sea all year round, often in the dark before dawn. I still feel wary of the water each time I get in it; but I also think of my first literary hero, Wilfred Owen, who shared my obsession.

Owen is known for his poems that dwelt on the pity and horror of war, but as a teenager his first verses were inspired by Hans Christian Andersen's *The Little Mermaid*. Owen's version, composed in his loopy handwriting in a cheap exercise book, summons up the 'exceeding deep' of the sea, with 'waggish dolphins turning somersault' and 'whales a-snorting fountains angrily'. The mermaid becomes infatuated with a handsome prince she sees sailing by; but it's hard not to see, now, a mask for Owen's own desires in the poem: for the prince with whom he, too, would like to fall in love.

As war came and he enlisted in the Artists Rifles, Owen still found time to return to the Tate Gallery and commune with his favourite painting, Herbert Draper's *Lament for Icarus* 1898. Icarus lies sprawled on a rock, having soared too near the sun with his waxen wings; his body is tanned by his foolhardy flight, and sea maidens bob up from

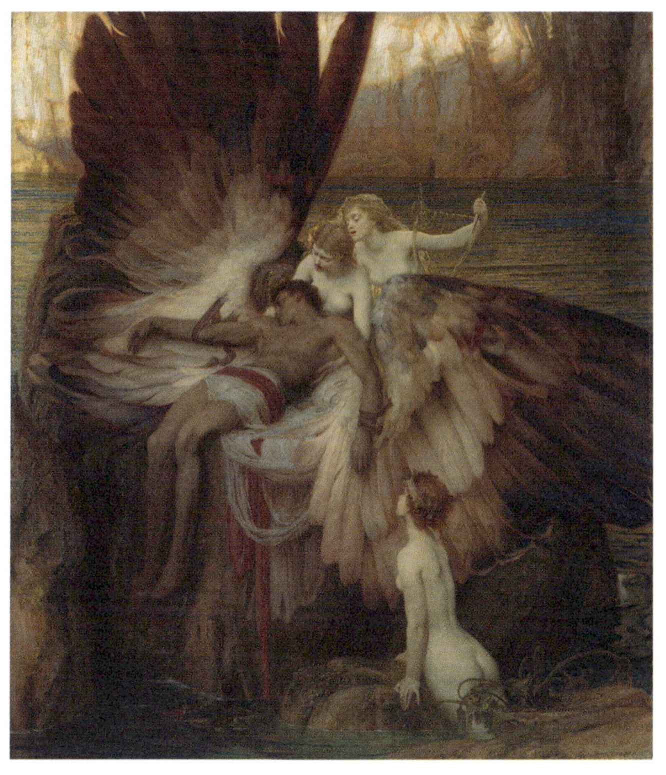

Herbert James Draper, *The Lament for Icarus* exhibited 1898, oil paint on canvas, 182.9 x 155.6, Tate

"THE SEA MARKS OUR PLACE IN TIME AND SPACE. IT'S WHERE WE CAME FROM AND WE'RE DRAWN TO IT, AS IF TO OUR OWN NATURAL HISTORY."

the waves to gaze upon his beautiful corpse. Owen saw himself, and his own future, in that picture, too. 'If I fall, I shall fall mightily', he told his mother. 'I shall be with Perseus and Icarus, whom I loved'.

Owen's last swim was on Folkestone beach, on the last day of summer, 1918. He waded into the surf in the company of a handsome soldier; his prince at last. But that afternoon Owen sailed across the English Channel for the battlefields of northern France. Three months later, six days before peace was declared, he was shot in a battle raging on the banks of a canal. One eyewitness account claimed that at the end, the young officer's body fell into the dark green water.

The sea is a mystery because we cannot see under what Herman Melville called 'the ocean's skin'. It seems to contain all our fears. It is as much darkness as it is light.

J.M.W. Turner's intense vision turned the sea from the calm classical composition of painters such as Claude Lorrain into something sensational and chaotic. Apocryphally, the artist himself claimed to have had his body strapped to a vessel's mast so that he could witness the sea in a storm. It was a sort of self-myth, with Turner as a pivotal point: the moment in which art altered the state of the sea in our heads. Turner incorporated the mayhem and uproar of industrial revolution into his art, and his late paintings of the sea become vortices, steam-powered or even electrified as much as acts of God. The humans in them are dwarfed by a new force not even the creator of these images could contain, least of all in his imagination.

Turner's romantic seas now acquire the power of political and environmental statements – from *The Slave Ship*, first exhibited in 1840, which may refer to the infamous *Zong*, a slave ship which in 1781 threw its human cargo overboard, discarded as so much ballast to be consumed by voracious monsters in the spumey waves, to a series of paintings depicting the premeditated slaughter

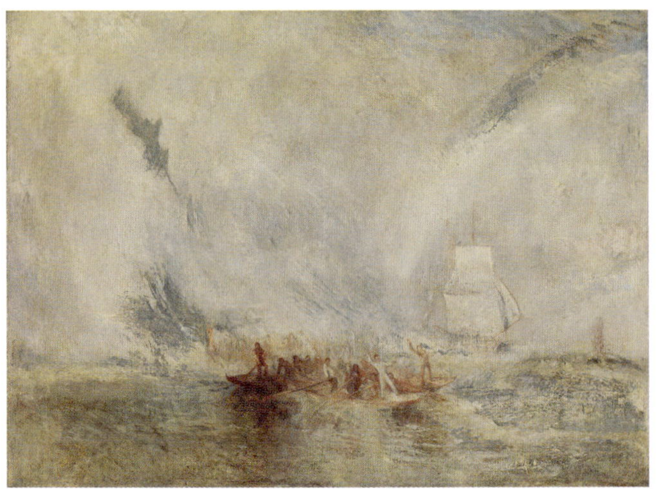

J.M.W. Turner, *Whalers* c.1845, oil paint on canvas, 130 x 161 x 18, Tate

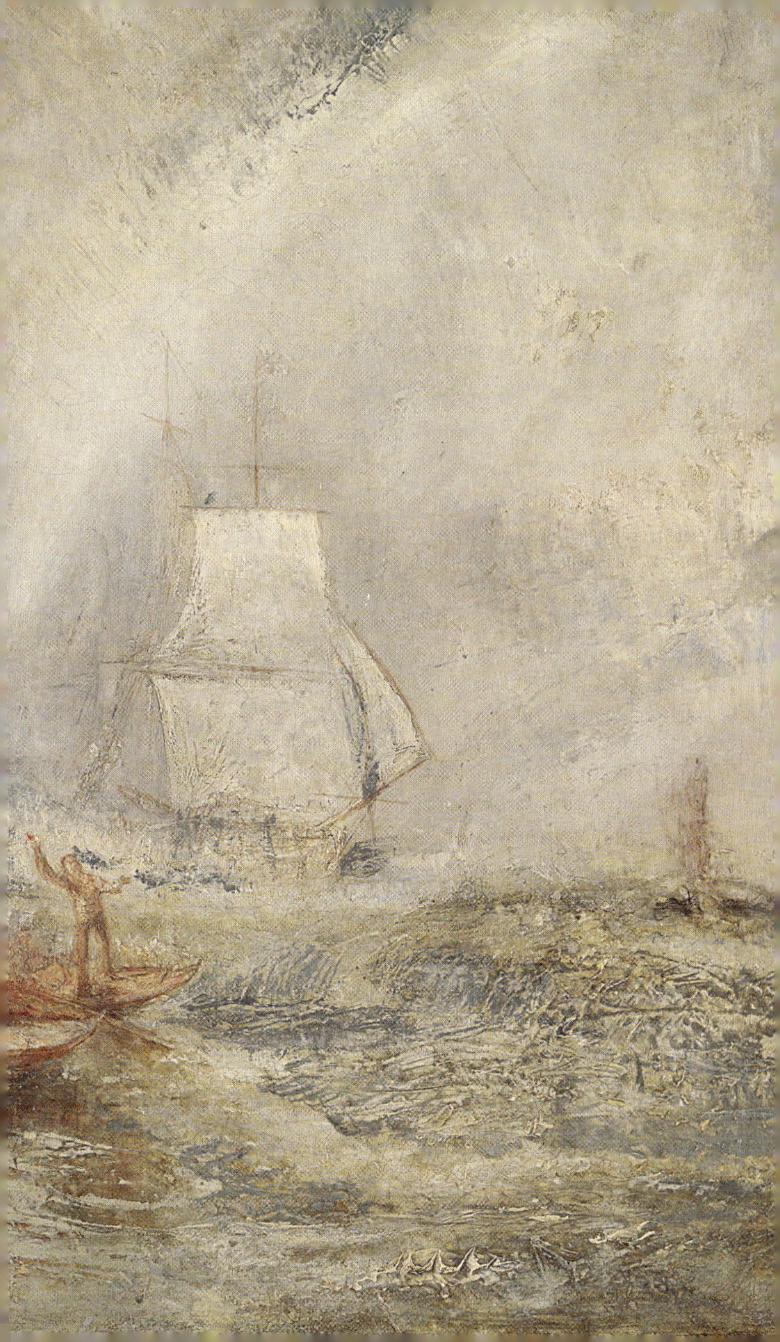

of leviathans which died to supply us with oil. As we stand in front of these pictures, they challenge us with our complicity. It was whale oil that lit and lubricated the remorseless engine of modern society. Whales lit the streets of London, Glasgow and Birmingham, Berlin, New York and Paris. Whales oiled the factories of the English Midlands and all points beyond in the mechanising western world. Indeed, Turner himself mixed his pigments with whale oil, thereby portraying dying animals with the very stuff produced by their demise. And his art, in turn, would inspire one of the greatest books about the sea ever written.

When the unreliable narrator of Melville's *Moby-Dick* – a young man who invites us to call him Ishmael – walks into a dark tavern in the whaling port of New Bedford on a snowy night, he is confronted in the entryway by 'a long, limber, portentous, black mass of something hovering in the centre of the picture ... floating in a nameless yeast.' It is clearly a Turner seascape: 'A boggy, soggy, squitchy picture truly, enough to drive a nervous man distracted ... a sort of indefinite, half-attained, unimaginable sublimity about it that fairly froze you to it, till you involuntarily took an oath with yourself to find out what that marvellous painting meant.'

"TURNER HIMSELF MIXED HIS PIGMENTS WITH WHALE OIL, THEREBY PORTRAYING DYING ANIMALS WITH THE VERY STUFF PRODUCED BY THEIR DEMISE."

The genesis of *Moby-Dick* lay partly in the author's visit to imperial London in 1849. His imagination had long been fired by fine art; now he saw Turner's paintings for real, and took that memory back across the Atlantic. But when it was published in 1851, the novel confounded Melville's contemporaries with its wild digressions, and it wasn't until the twentieth century that it was seen as a revolutionary work of art. In 1923, D.H. Lawrence declared Melville was 'a futurist long before futurism found paint', and *Moby-Dick* influenced modernist writers from Marianne Moore and James Joyce to T.E. Lawrence and W.H. Auden. Virginia Woolf read the book three times, and you can hear its echoes in her own novels *To the Lighthouse*, *Orlando* and *The Waves* (though she said that no one would suspect her work was inspired by 'my vision of a fin rising on a wide blank sea'). She even nicknamed her lover, Vita Sackville-West, 'my porpoise'.

Melville, with his own ambivalent sexuality, was the great poet of the ocean even if, like his fellow novelist Joseph Conrad, he could not make up his mind whether he loved or hated it. With its passages on the 'appalling whiteness of the whale' as an allegory of the abuses of slavery, and its almost abstract images evoking the disastrous effects of western domination on the natural world, *Moby-Dick* became a seminal work, spawning a new myth of the sea.

Ishmael will go on to discover the meaning of that painting; but for every other character in the book, the narrative that follows spells calamity – one which has been seen by commentators from C.L.R. James to Edward Said as a metaphor for a world thrown out of kilter by madness, inhumanity and greed.

The art of Turner and Melville bore witness to the changing meaning of the sea. Under our human sway, it shifted from creation myth to economic resource, from faith to exploitation. Transition is the default state of the sea, as it seems to speed up evolution before our eyes. From the ancient to the medieval to the modernist sea, it throws up strange things, then takes them back and turns them into something else. Hardness and preciousness intertwine: pearls form from grit in the silky white interiors of oysters; squids boast beaks like parrots; slipper shells form gender-shifting towers, one atop the other, from young males to older females at the bottom. But the sea's rarest substance is its most alchemical: ambergris, a cholesterol produced in the stomachs of sperm whales before being expelled into the water where it matures and acquires a heady scent that is still the basis of luxurious perfumes.

Surrealist artists have always looked to the sea and its rites of watery transubstantiation and subversive conjunctions. The artist Eileen Agar in particular drew on this synergy, as she worked with found objects from the beach. By placing a convoluted whelk shell on top of a sea urchin, for instance, she evoked a specimen from a baroque cabinet of curiosities, or some weird new chimera from the future. Mischievous and playful, Agar extended her art to herself, making hats out of crustacean carapaces and sticking cockle shells to a human skull she had painted gold, inspired by Shakespeare's *The Tempest*, in which a drowned duke's bones turn to coral and his eyes to pearls. She saw the human body as a part of a performance enacted between the rocks and tides, between the apparent safety of the land and the deep mystery of the sea.

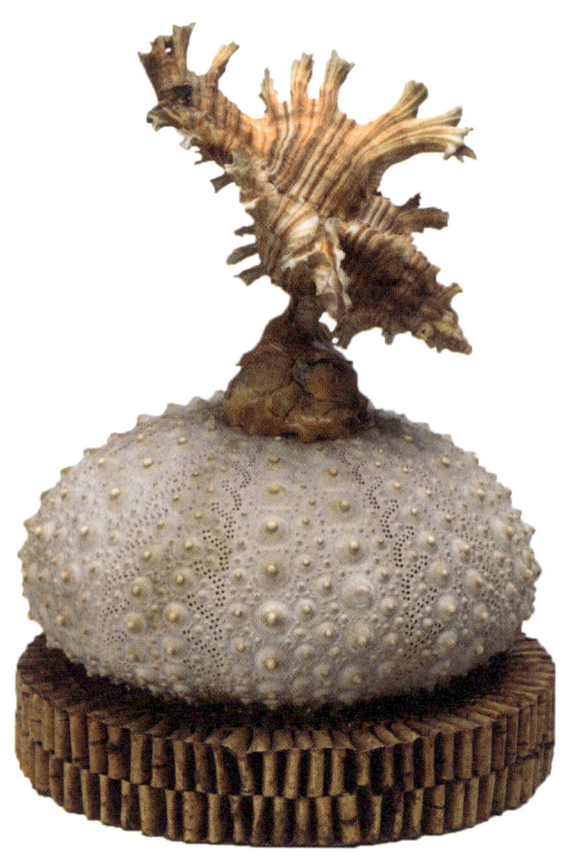

Eileen Agar, *Sculpture consisting of a shell stuck on top of sea urchin mounted on a base made out of woven bark*, date unknown, shell and wood, 14.5 x 10 x 10, Tate

"SHE SAW THE HUMAN BODY AS A PART OF A PERFORMANCE BETWEEN THE APPARENT SAFETY OF THE LAND AND THE DEEP MYSTERY OF THE SEA."

In the summer of 1935, Agar was staying by the seaside in Swanage, on the Isle of Purbeck in Dorset, when she met Paul Nash, who was also spending the summer there. Though both were with their respective partners, the two artists fell in love, united by their passion for the sea. Nash had a certain allure, Agar said; he would bring her strange stones and marked pebbles he had picked up from the beach, laying them before her like a penguin, he joked. The pair began to collaborate on designs for veneers and 'other matters of aesthetic decision'. Nash described her lover's ebullient art as 'entire, almost Agar Agar'.

The following year, Nash would publish his essay 'Swanage, or Seaside Surrealism' in the *Architectural*

Review. In it, he noted that the resort, which began as the haunt of prehistoric turtles and crocodiles, had ended up as a place 'of doubtful enchantment, a grotesque made awe-inspiring by indefinition'. The inhabitants, Nash fantasised, couldn't bear the ugliness of the Victorian resort, and instead looked away, seeking solace by gazing out to the uncluttered sea.

Of course, both Nash and Agar fed on such eccentricities. In Swanage, Agar gathered up all sorts of charged things. She was especially proud of a 'crucifix fish' – a catfish skull traditionally said to represent the form of the crucified Christ. And in the nearby cove at Lulworth, Agar 'unpebbled a long snakey monster with a bird's beak' and a rusty anchor chain 'metamorphosed by the sea into a new creation'. Both of these finds were photographed by Nash and incorporated into an evocative collage in which Agar's sea monster looms over the bay, terrifying a lone swan riding against the tide, while a pearly moon rises over the clouds, having apparently drifted there from a painting by William Blake.

Like a surrealist postcard sent to themselves, this dream-composition became a emblem of the affair between the two artists. Nash loved Agar's gold and bundled hair; she returned his creative trust.

'There was an almost unconscious to and fro-ness between us', she said, 'which continued until he died'.

In the summer of 1972, the artist Derek Jarman set off for Dorset, a place he'd known from childhood holidays, but also from the work of Nash and Agar, which he loved. Jarman and his collaborators – the artist Andrew Logan, two art students, Marc Balet and Bente Lohse, and a young man known only as Ian – arrived on the Isle of Purbeck to make a short film Jarman had devised. Its title was *The Siren and the Sailor*; it was later known as *At Low Tide*.

In the silent sequence – our imaginations supply the soundtrack of rushing waves – we follow the Super 8mm lens panning up the rocks to find Logan standing there. He's dressed as a sea god in a gold and silver mask made by Jarman's collaborator, Christopher Hobbs; draped over his arms like translucent pink and green seaweed is a tattered wrap fashioned from the ballgown Logan had worn for his first Alternative Miss World show, staged earlier that year in his Hackney studio.

The film's colours are bright and saturated with 1970s glamour; the sea glitters in the sun. Slowly the sea god stalks over the rocks to find the siren, naked save for a fishing net wrapped round her, singing her fatal song. In a rock pool at her feet

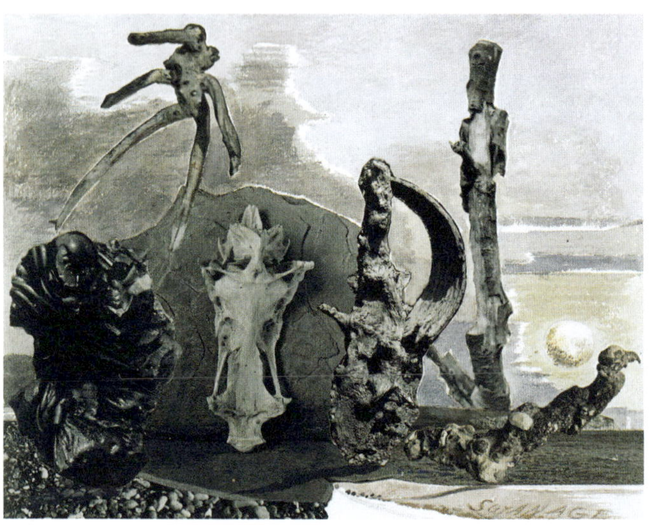

Paul Nash, *Swanage* c.1936, graphite, watercolour and photographs, black and white, on paper, 53.5 x 63.4 x 2.2, Tate

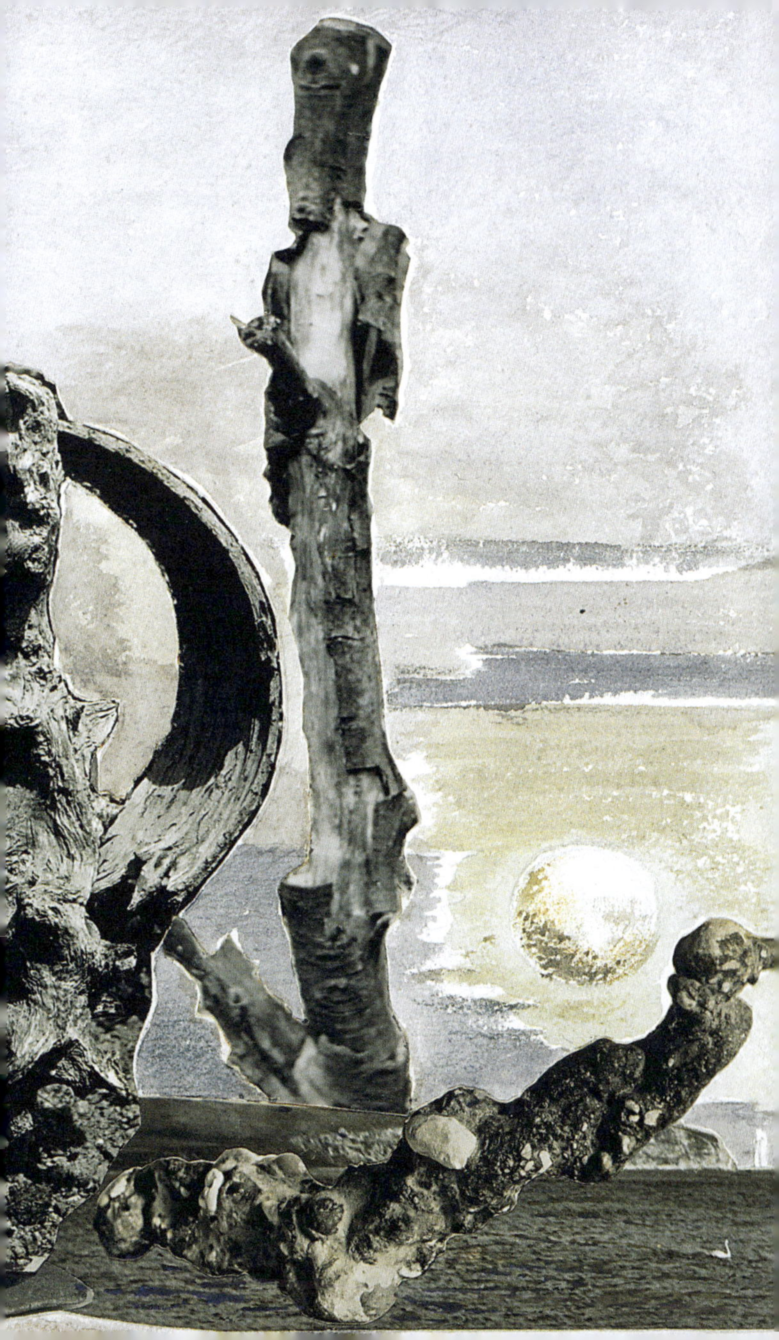

floats her victim: a drowned sailor. He's clad only in white bell bottom trousers, like Melville's handsome sailor Billy Budd or Draper's fallen Icarus. The whole production is a pantomime, an augury of the staged performances, album covers and films of musicians such as David Bowie and Roxy Music. It has the air of an innocent decadence in which the sea embodies a shifting sense of possibilities, wrapped up not just in Jarman's nostalgia for his own past but in the fantasies of his films to come.

In the summer of 1987, newly diagnosed with HIV and seeking an escape from the suffocating city of London, Jarman acquired a tarry black hut on the shingle expanse of Dungeness on the Kentish coast. He called it Prospect Cottage, and set about creating a magical garden around it. With its stone necklaces, spiky plants, rusty forks, bits of driftwood and shards from a shattered lighthouse lens, Jarman's plot blurred with the shingle and the sea, a tidal place in history. Its setting, like its creator, evoked Prospero's island of strange noises in *The Tempest*; but it also acted as a dark mirror of Jarman's 'modern nature', a phrase coined by his friend, the artist Maggi Hambling.

This term reflected the natural world to which Jarman had returned, but also the modern nature of his queer identity, shaped in part by his political

"SLOWLY THE SEA GOD STALKS OVER THE ROCKS TO FIND THE SIREN SINGING HER FATAL SONG. IN A ROCK POOL AT HER FEET FLOATS HER VICTIM: A DROWNED SAILOR."

outrage and in part by the looming Dungeness B nuclear power station which glowed at night as if with the radiation inside. As his body tried to deal with its viral invaders with the aid of chemotherapy, Jarman's garden embodied his resistance and persistence. In a poem to future visitors, he hoped its stony shrines would 'perform an archaeology of soul', as memories 'of our vanished days / here – at the sea's edge'.

The artist was looking beyond his own mortality to an elementally changed world. The distant sea that Jarman saw from his window as a line on the horizon is the same shore that now receives refugees from across the Channel. In her painting *2016* 2016, Hambling depicts a submerged boat just visible

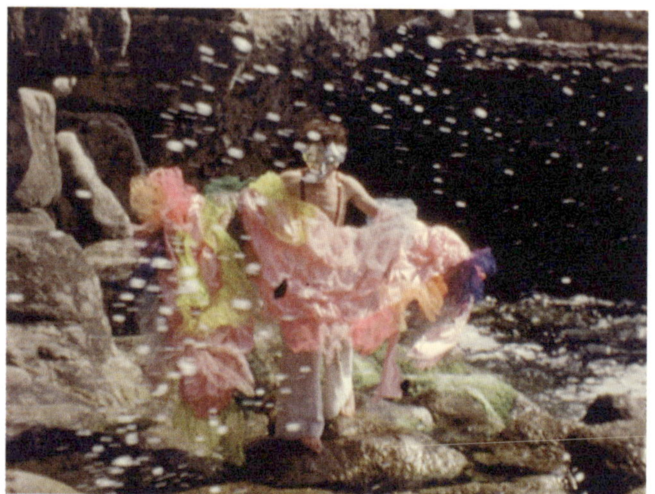

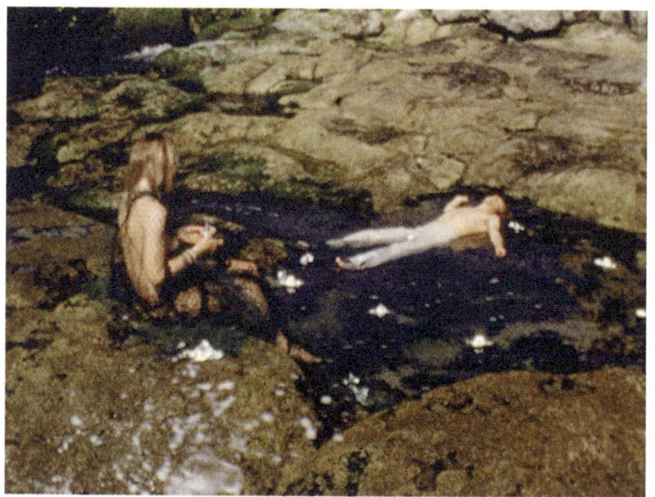

Derek Jarman, *At Low Tide (The Siren and the Sailor)*, film stills, 1972

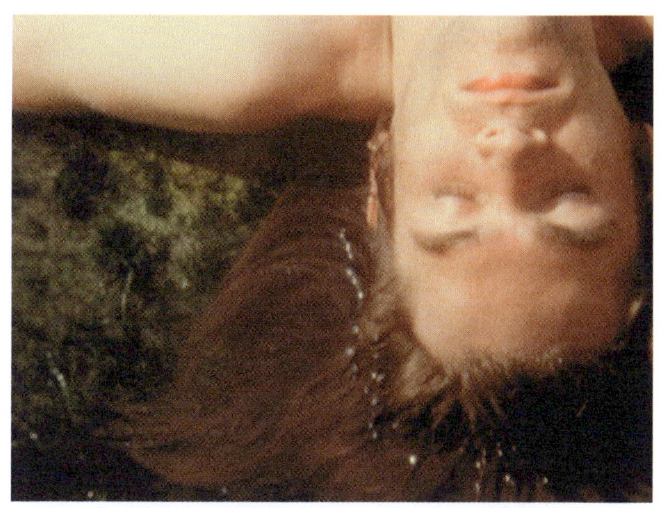

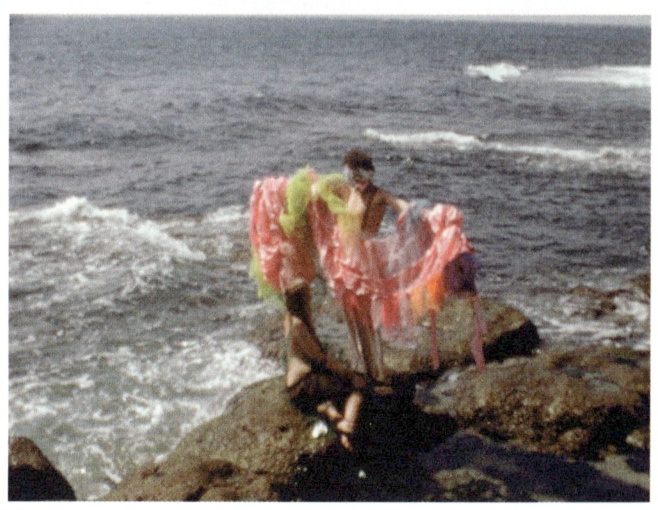

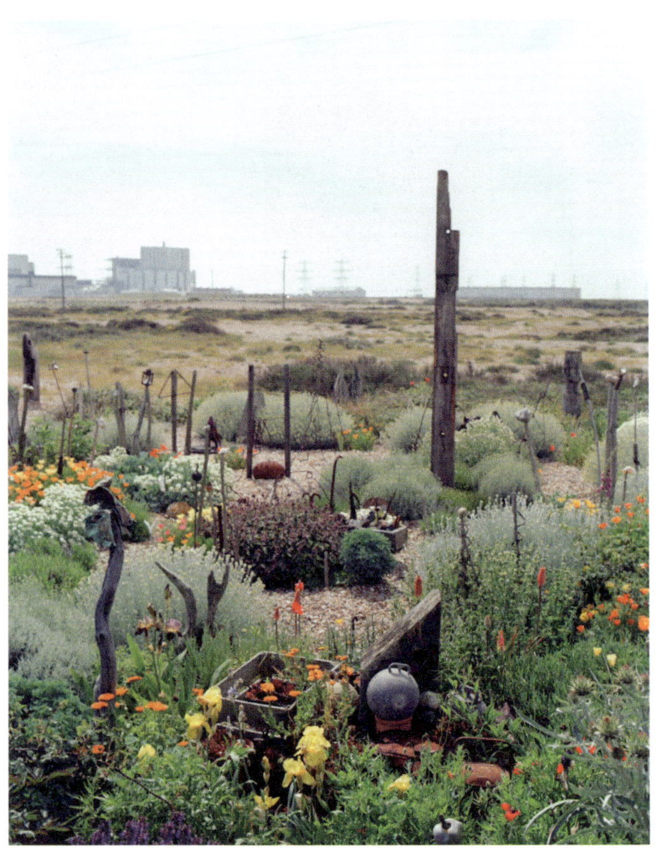

Howard Sooley, *Prospect Cottage* 1995

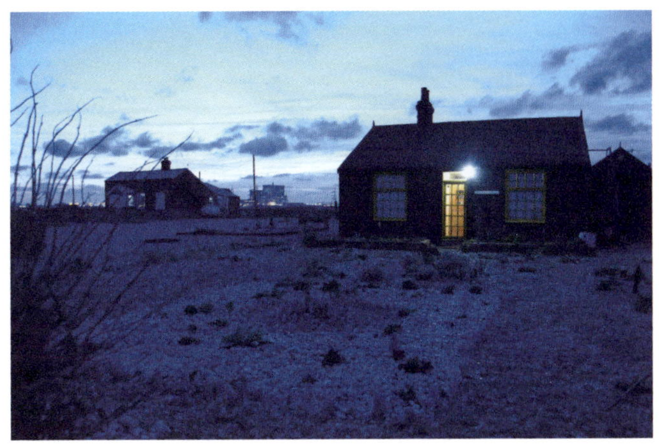

Philip Hoare, *Prospect Cottage*, November 2019

"THE DISTANT SEA THAT JARMAN SAW FROM HIS WINDOW AS A LINE ON THE HORIZON IS THE SAME SHORE THAT NOW RECEIVES REFUGEES FROM ACROSS THE CHANNEL."

beneath the sea's rising surface. The apparent calmness, even beauty, of the layered image, with the sun shining down on it, only intensifies its horror. We hear the whirr of the helicopter blades as the press photographers hover over the scene, but from the sea there is only silence. As the poet Marianne Moore wrote, 'the sea has nothing to give but a well excavated grave.'

The sea and the shore have ever been places of life and death; of siren voices and ideas. In Colin Self's *Power and Beauty* series of 1968, the British pop artist screenprinted an image of a dead whale on a beach, almost mockingly tinted an oceanic blue. The rorqual pleats of the mammal's belly here take on an architectural immensity: it's a Warhol disaster, a stranded alien dragged from a crashed UFO. As the animal's open mouth utters a voiceless cry, Newton might be there beside it, taking account of the disaster. He cannot measure what we have lost – the three million great whales killed in the twentieth century alone – nor tell us of the colour of the water or our own futility.

Self's print was a reaction to the environmental movements of the sixties in which the whale became an icon of both hope and despair. Britain was still engaged in the whaling industry, out of sight in the Southern and South Atlantic oceans; men working on those ships claimed they would never have been able to do their job if the whales had been able to scream. All this to provide oil, cosmetics and margarine; the bones of these giants did not become coral, but were ground up as rose fertiliser. Their guts strung tennis racquets. Our mothers wore whale lipstick while we ate whale-spread sandwiches and the family dog munched on tinned whale.

At precisely this same time, a pair of young scientists, Roger Payne and Scott McVay, were taping the songs of humpback whales out in the Atlantic Ocean. They had been alerted to the eerie sounds by sonic arrays laid by the US Navy to detect enemy submarines. Payne's recordings of what he called a sound as big

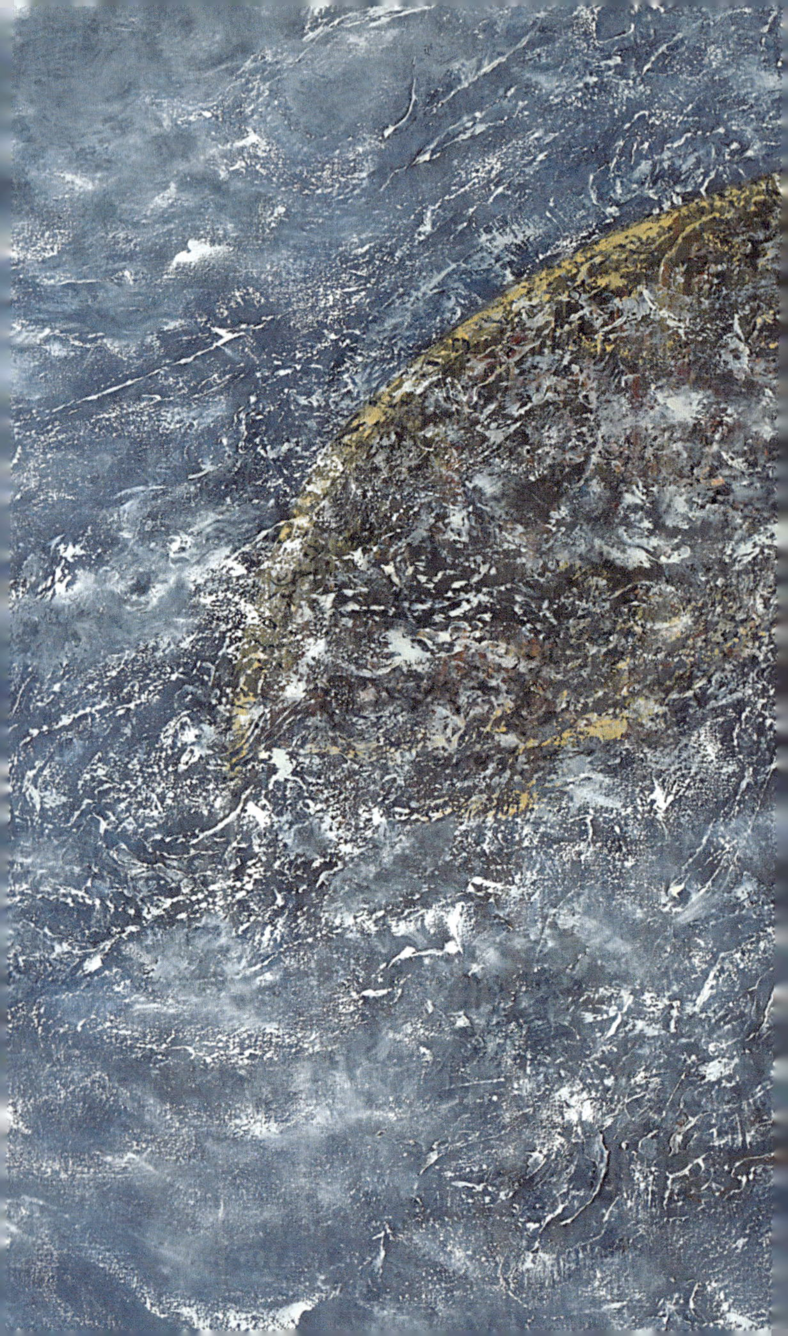

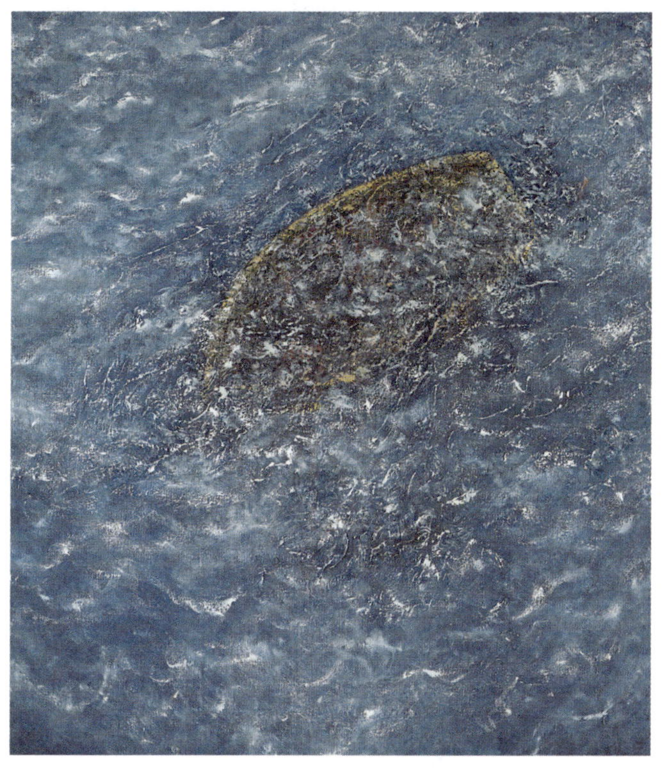

Maggi Hambling, *2016* 2016, oil paint on canvas, 213.5 x 182.7, Tate

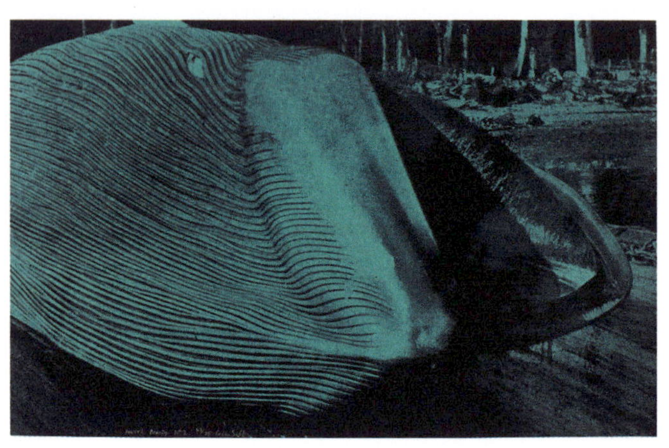

Colin Self, *Power and Beauty No. 2* 1968, screenprint on paper, 67.9 x 104.3, Tate

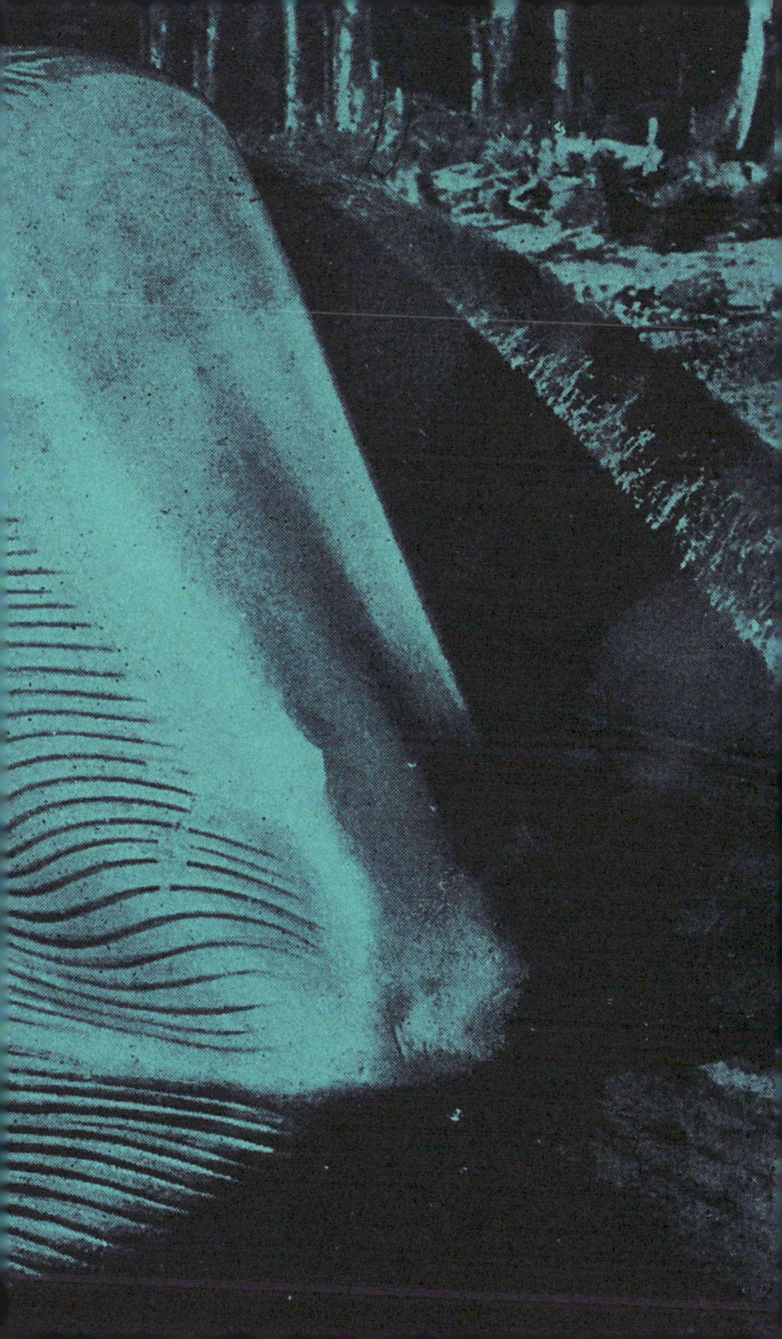

"OUR MOTHERS WORE WHALE LIPSTICK WHILE WE ATE WHALE-SPREAD SANDWICHES AND THE FAMILY DOG MUNCHED ON TINNED WHALE."

as the sea suddenly gave a voice to supposedly dumb animals. Released as a bestselling record in the 1970s, they changed the future: we realised that whales also had a culture, an art, and that they seemed, in their poetic lament, to be protesting their abuse.

Their art saved the whales. In 1983, an international moratorium called a halt on the hunting of the creature; the remorseless cull was stalled. Now, in the twenty-first century, populations of humpbacks are expanding in oceans where encounters with humans were once fatal for them, and new techniques promise that we may soon discover the meanings of their vocalisations.

But will we want to hear what they have to say? Other siren voices have come into play: seismic surveys for oil and gas, sonar exercises by the world's navies; the pandemonium of the noise of modern marine traffic. All conspire to create an inhospitable environment for animals whose greatest sense is that of sound. The contemporary artist Angela Cockayne portrays this dilemma in a blueprint that seems made from the sea itself, in which the whale is divided up phrenologically – as if, in our eagerness to follow the cause of enlightenment, we had somehow lost our way as we placed people, animals, ideas and cultures in boxes, with the relevant labels attached; as if the chaos of creation looked tidier that way.

Will we save ourselves from the sea? For centuries it has acted as a carbon sink, a cistern of our sins, absorbing our emissions via ancient reserves which are themselves the products of primordial seas. Our actions threaten to acidify and overheat it; we plunder even the deepest ocean bed to sustain our headlong progress. And now, in this century, it is set to rise up against us.

Yet for all that we have done to it, the sea still offers a sense of possibility. It knows no national boundaries. The oceans connect us, rather than keep us apart. 'The sea, the great unifier, is man's

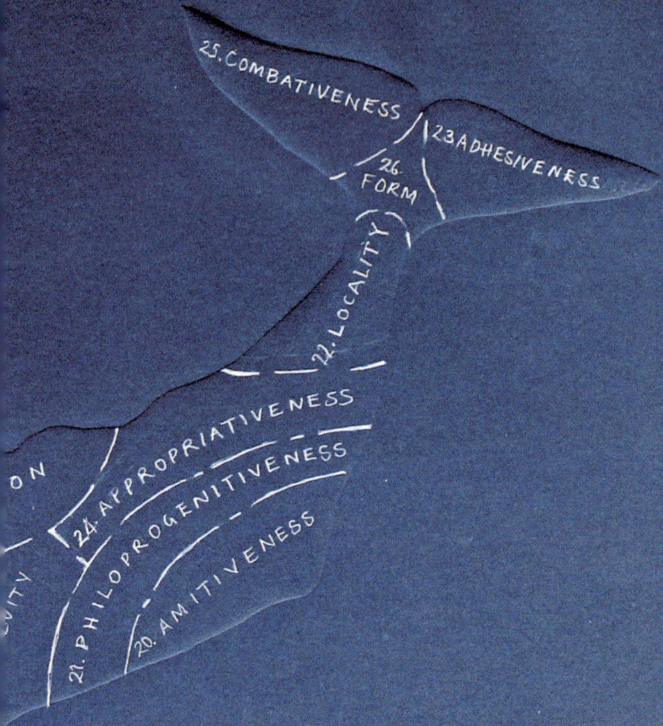

25. COMBATIVENESS

23. ADHESIVENESS

26. FORM

22. LOCALITY

24. APPROPRIATIVENESS

21. PHILOPROGENITIVENESS

20. AMITIVENESS

ON

ITY

Fig 1. Phrenology of Cachelot

1. Kindness, goodness.
2. Intuition - spiritual revery
3. Ocean bed to outerspace.
4. Grandeur.
5. Appetite, hunger.
6. Accumulation.
7. Measure of all things.
8. sympathy for suffering
9. motive, rational coherence.
10. Memory of facts.
11. Understanding of situation.
12. Ability to understand.
13. Communication, expression
14. Thoughts & action based on emotion
15. Prudence, provision.
16. Cause to effect.
17. Observation.
18. Cognizance of time.
19. Respect.
20. Sexual connubial love.
21. Parental love.
22. Recollection of place.
23. Friendship, sociability
24. Ambition, display.
25. Resistance, defense.
26. Recollection of shape.

(Largest brain on Earth)

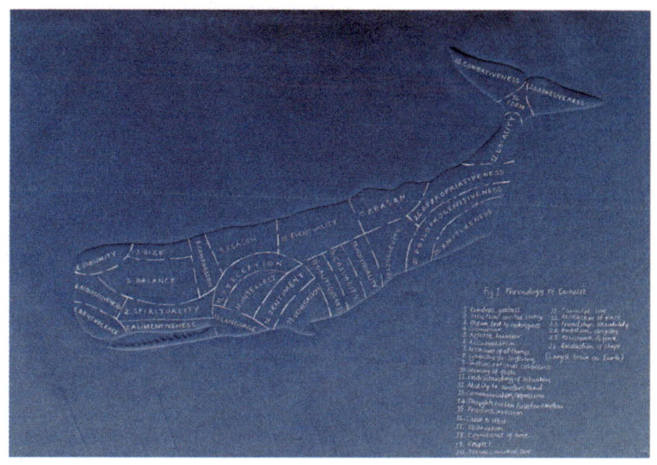

Angela Cockayne, *Phrenology* 2009, giclee blueprint from an embossed drawing, 420 x 594, Tate

"THERE'S A SENSE OF TRUST AND ADVENTURE, FULL OF THE EXCITEMENT AND TREPIDATION OF THE SEA. IN A MOMENT MELANIE WILL LET GO, AND HER LEGS KICK FREE."

only hope', as Jacques Cousteau said. Its bright blue, steel-grey, bean-green waters, are a promise renewed with each tide. An act of faith, without which neither you nor I could survive.

When I was a boy, my mother told me about a big old Victorian cast-iron tub in her childhood home, along the side of which my grandfather had painted a spouting whale to cheer it up. That image made me fear the sea so much I didn't even like taking a bath. The sight of my own body in the water made me think of deep-sea fishes ready to grab at me with toothed jaws bigger than themselves.

Now I see it another way.

In the summer of 1976, the artist Michael Andrew took his six year-old daughter Melanie swimming off a rocky shore in Scotland. Two years later, Andrew made a painting based on a photograph taken at the time. He later recalled that he painted the image as life-size, so that the figures should feel real to him.

Melanie's hands are tight in her father's grip. The deep darkness is below, the bright light above. There's a sense of trust and adventure, full of the excitement and trepidation of the sea.

In a moment Melanie will let go, and her legs kick free. Her arms will reach out and her body will be borne up by the body of the sea.

By all the seas that ever were, and all the seas that will ever be.

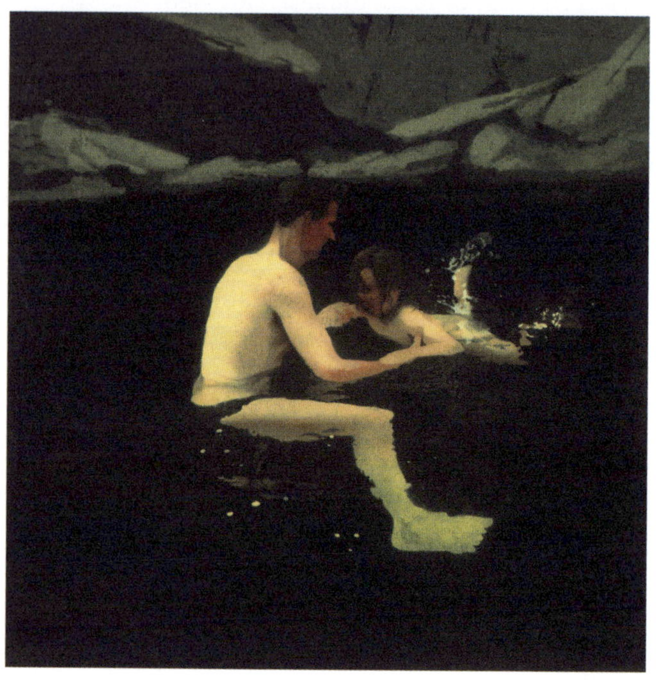

Michael Andrews, *Melanie and Me Swimming* 1978–9, acrylic paint on canvas, 182.9 x 182.9, Tate

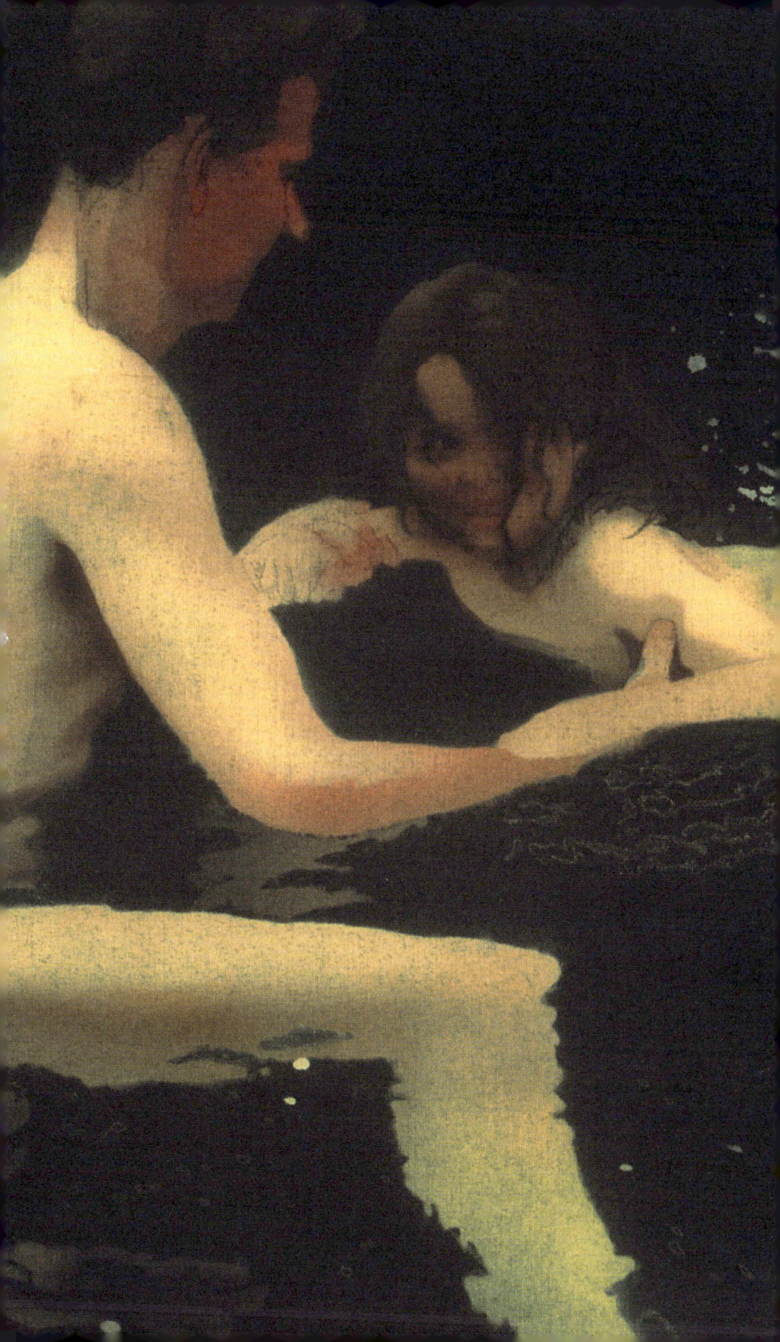